DAYS THAT SHOOK THE WORLD

THE CHERNOBYL DISASTER

APRIL 26, 1986

Paul Dowswell

RAINTREE
STECK-VAUGHN
PUBLISHERS

A Harcourt Company

Austin New York
www.raintreesteckvaughn.com

DAYS THAT SHOOK THE WORLD

Published by Raintree Steck-Vaughn Publishers,
an imprint of Steck-Vaughn Company

Library of Congress Cataloging-in-Publication Data is available upon request.

ISBN 0-7398-6049-6

Printed in Italy. Bound in the United States.

1 2 3 4 5 6 7 8 9 0 LB 06 05 04 03 02

Picture Acknowledgments:

Cover picture: A technician checks the level of radiation around the shattered reactor at Chernobyl (Popperfoto/Reuters).

Title page picture: Chernobyl workers pose in front of the reactor after the disaster (Popperfoto/Reuters).

We are grateful to the following for permission to reproduce photographs:
Associated Press 42 (Victor Pobedinsky), 46 (Efrem Lukatsky); Corbis 8; Corbis Sygma 32 (Kostin Igor); JVZ Picture Library 24 (Vaughan Melzer); Novosti (London) 7, 18,19, 20, 25, 26, 31, 33, 35, 36; Popperfoto 11 (Reuters), 12, 17 (Reuters), 21, 29 (Reuters), 33, (Reuters), 39 (Reuters), 41 (Reuters); Rex Features 6, 15 (Sipa Press), 16 (Sipa Press), 37 (Sipa Press/Heidi Bradner), 40 (Sipa Press/Wojtel Laski), 42-43 (Sipa Press/Heidi Bradner); Science Photo Library 10 (Alex Bartel), 30 (Novosti), 38 (Lawrence Livermore Laboratory); Still Pictures 13 (Sabine Vielmo); Topham Picturepoint 9 (Photri), 14, 23, 27 (Novosti), 28 (AP), 34, 37, 45.

CONTENTS

The Chernobyl power plant before the disaster of April 26, 1986.

Friday, April 25, 1986, was a fine spring day at the V. I. Lenin nuclear power plant at Chernobyl, Ukraine, with clear blue skies and a crisp, fresh breeze blowing in from the Kiev Reservoir. The workers at the plant lived good lives, comfortably housed with their families in the thriving communities of nearby Pripyat and Chernobyl town. They were conveniently located for the daily trip to the power plant: Pripyat was 1.9 miles (3 km) away and Chernobyl town was 5.6 miles (9 km). The workers' commute was brief, and took them through the pleasant Ukrainian countryside.

Under the command of station director Victor Brukhanov, the power plant was the largest of its kind in the world, and one of the Soviet Union's proudest technological achievements. Its name alone (for the Russian Revolution's communist leader, Vladimir Ilyich Lenin) made the link between Chernobyl and the political philosophy of the Soviet Union clear to all. At the entrance to the plant a billboard proclaimed: "The Party of Lenin, the power of the people...will lead us to victory." Along one wall, in huge letters, ran the slogan "Communism will triumph."

A Moment in Time

In the No. 4 reactor control room at 2:00 P.M., white-coated technicians begin the complex procedure of shutting down the reactor. Concentrating hard on instrument dials and computer printouts, they pull levers and press buttons to start the process. But a phone call from the controller of the electricity supply to Kiev requests that the reactor be kept working to prevent power cuts in the city, as demand for electricity is very high. The technicians have no idea what a lucky escape this phone call provides. Without the delay, the test would have been conducted during the day, and the staff would have been in the middle of one of the greatest industrial accidents of all time. Instead, that terrible situation is reserved for the shift that follows them.

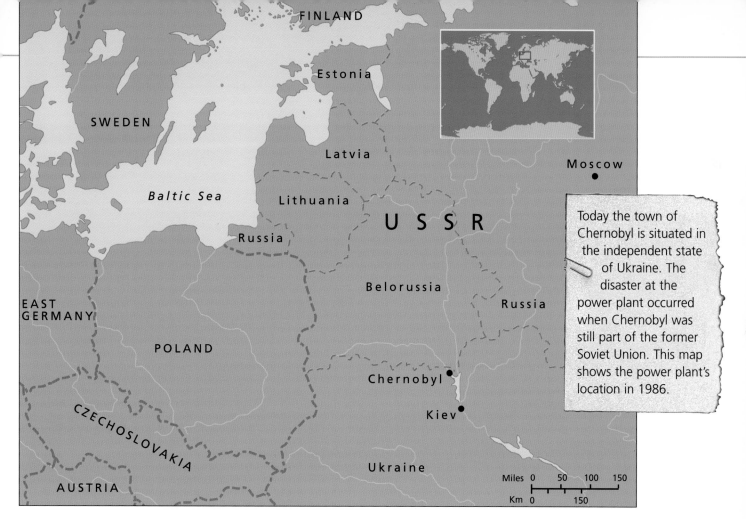

FINLAND

Estonia

SWEDEN

Latvia

Baltic Sea

Lithuania

U S S R

Russia

Moscow
•

EAST
GERMANY

Belorussia

Russia

POLAND

CZECHOSLOVAKIA

Chernobyl •

Kiev •

AUSTRIA

Ukraine

| Miles | 0 | 50 | 100 | 150 |
| Km | 0 | | 150 | |

Today the town of Chernobyl is situated in the independent state of Ukraine. The disaster at the power plant occurred when Chernobyl was still part of the former Soviet Union. This map shows the power plant's location in 1986.

On April 25, 1986, the No. 4 reactor was scheduled to be shut down for routine maintenance. Chief engineer Nikolai Fomin decided to take advantage of this to test a safety procedure during the shutdown operation, when the reactor was still working. Tests would be run to check whether, in the event of a total loss of electrical power, the plant could continue to function with the emergency electrical power supplied by the momentum of rapidly spinning generator turbine blades. This power was especially necessary for the pumps that supplied water to cool the reactor. To carry out the test realistically, the emergency reactor core cooling system needed to be switched off.

What no one realized at the time, sadly, was that this experiment was sowing the seeds of a nuclear disaster that would turn hundreds of thousands of lives upside down and contribute in a major way to the collapse of the Soviet Union. But there was no reason why anyone should. Government propaganda had convinced Soviet citizens that Chernobyl was so safe that the likelihood of an accident was ten million to one. None of them had the slightest inkling that this beautiful day would be the last of its kind in their lives.

The modern town of Pripyat was built especially for Chernobyl's workforce.

Nuclear power can be used for both peaceful and warlike ends. This atomic bomb explosion at Bikinii Atoll in 1954 shows the awesome power of a nuclear blast.

EVERYTHING IN THE WORLD is made of minute particles called atoms. These particles are so tiny that there are more atoms in an ant than there are people in the world. Nuclear power is made by splitting (breaking up) the atoms of a particular metal called uranium. When the nucleus (center) of a uranium atom is split, it gives off heat. Splitting the nucleus also causes other surrounding uranium atoms to split, in what is called a "nuclear reaction."

The energy in an atom can be released in two ways— in the massively powerful explosion of a nuclear bomb, or in the steady, controlled flow produced by a nuclear reactor. The stupendous strength of nuclear power first became known to the world in 1945, when two atomic bombs were dropped on Japan to end World War II. Before then, scientists working in

conditions of utmost secrecy under the direction of Italian physicist Enrico Fermi had created a controlled nuclear reaction in the world's first nuclear reactor at the University of Chicago in 1942. In 1951, the nuclear energy in an experimental reactor at Idaho Falls was harnessed to produce electricity. The heat generated by nuclear reaction was used to make steam to turn a turbine. Then, in 1956, the world's first nuclear power plant, at Calder Hall, Cumbria, in England, began to produce electricity for national consumption.

Today there are more than 400 nuclear reactors producing electricity around the world. The most common type is known as a thermal reactor. The reactor at Chernobyl was a thermal reactor. You can see how one works in the diagram on the opposite page.

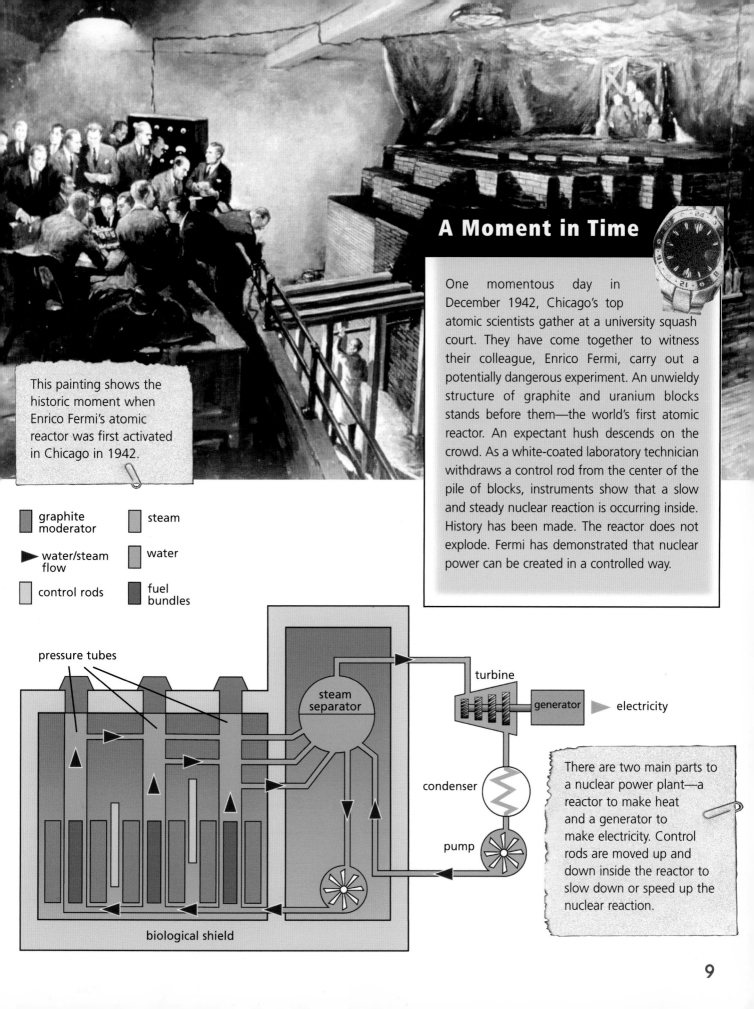

This painting shows the historic moment when Enrico Fermi's atomic reactor was first activated in Chicago in 1942.

A Moment in Time

One momentous day in December 1942, Chicago's top atomic scientists gather at a university squash court. They have come together to witness their colleague, Enrico Fermi, carry out a potentially dangerous experiment. An unwieldy structure of graphite and uranium blocks stands before them—the world's first atomic reactor. An expectant hush descends on the crowd. As a white-coated laboratory technician withdraws a control rod from the center of the pile of blocks, instruments show that a slow and steady nuclear reaction is occurring inside. History has been made. The reactor does not explode. Fermi has demonstrated that nuclear power can be created in a controlled way.

graphite moderator

steam

water/steam flow

water

control rods

fuel bundles

pressure tubes

steam separator

turbine

generator

electricity

condenser

pump

biological shield

There are two main parts to a nuclear power plant—a reactor to make heat and a generator to make electricity. Control rods are moved up and down inside the reactor to slow down or speed up the nuclear reaction.

Nuclear Energy and Weapons

Nuclear weapons use a radioactive metal called plutonium as their source of explosive energy. In its natural state, plutonium is extremely scarce, but it is a by-product of the uranium fuel used in nuclear reactors.

One of the reasons that many countries adopted nuclear power as a source of energy was to gain access to sources of plutonium for nuclear weapons.

WHEN THE IDEA OF using nuclear power to provide energy was first unveiled, one British politician excitedly described it as "power so cheap it would not even be metered." The phrase caught on, and many people imagined a future where they would never again have to worry about paying their electric bills.

Nuclear power has many advantages. If nuclear power stations work without mishap, they are much cleaner environmentally than the "fossil fuels" of coal, gas, or oil used in nonnuclear power plants. When they burn, these "dirtier" types of fuel release harmful gases, which pollute the atmosphere and contribute to acid rain and global warming. Also, such fossil fuels will run out soon. Oil and gas, for example, are being used up so quickly that scientists predict the earth's supply will be exhausted by the middle of this century. Coal supplies may last another 400 years. The earth's supply of uranium, the principal fuel of a nuclear reactor, will also run out eventually. But a piece of uranium the size

A modern nuclear power plant at Indian Point, New York. Each dome contains a nuclear reactor.

of a pin contains as much energy as 5,000 tons of coal, so it seems likely that uranium will be used up at a much slower rate.

However, the advantages of nuclear power are offset by considerable risks. When atoms are split in a nuclear reaction, they send off invisible rays called radiation. These rays are very harmful to living things, and may cause burns, cancer, and other ailments. Because of this, nuclear reactors must be built and run to very exacting safety standards—if things go wrong, the consequences can be catastrophic. This is expensive; a new reactor costs in the area of three billion dollars. A major fire at a fossil fuel power plant may cause local problems, but a similar disaster at a nuclear power plant could affect neighboring continents, not to mention countries. Nuclear power plants also produce nuclear waste in the form of spent fuel rods. Such waste is highly radioactive, and continues to be so for 150,000 years. It has to be stored safely out of harm's way, and this increases the expense of producing nuclear energy.

Radiation and Living Things

Radiation in extreme doses, for example from a nuclear accident or weapon, can kill very rapidly. But low-level exposure over many years may also be fatal.

Extreme exposure causes the disintegration of skin, bones, and internal organs, and results in agonizing death over days or weeks.

Low-level exposure causes mutations to DNA. This leads to birth defects such as mental retardation, or higher susceptibility to leukemia, sterility, cancer (especially of thyroid, breast, and lung), and bone-marrow damage, resulting in the loss of the ability to fight disease.

Antinuclear protesters from the Greenpeace environmental pressure group demonstrate against nuclear waste.

IT WAS ALWAYS A LITTLE unlikely that a physical reaction that produced something as awesomely destructive as a nuclear bomb could also be used in a totally safe way to drive a power plant. Nuclear power plants never did live up to the promise of "power so cheap it would not even be metered," and practical problems arising from producing energy in this way were both inevitable and expensive to overcome. The history of nuclear accidents is a shadowy one. Great secrecy has always surrounded the production of nuclear fuel because of its direct link with nuclear weapons.

In the United States during the 1950s and 1960s, minor accidents in experimental reactors occurred. In 1971, 53,000 gallons (200,000 l) of radioactive-contaminated water were released into the Mississippi River in Minnesota. Most serious of all, in March 1979 at Three Mile Island nuclear power plant in Pennsylvania, the reactor core melted and radioactive gases and liquid waste were released into the environment. A total of 80,000 people living nearby had to leave their homes. The "meltdown" occurred because the pumps providing water to cool the reactor failed, and technicians made mistakes trying to correct this.

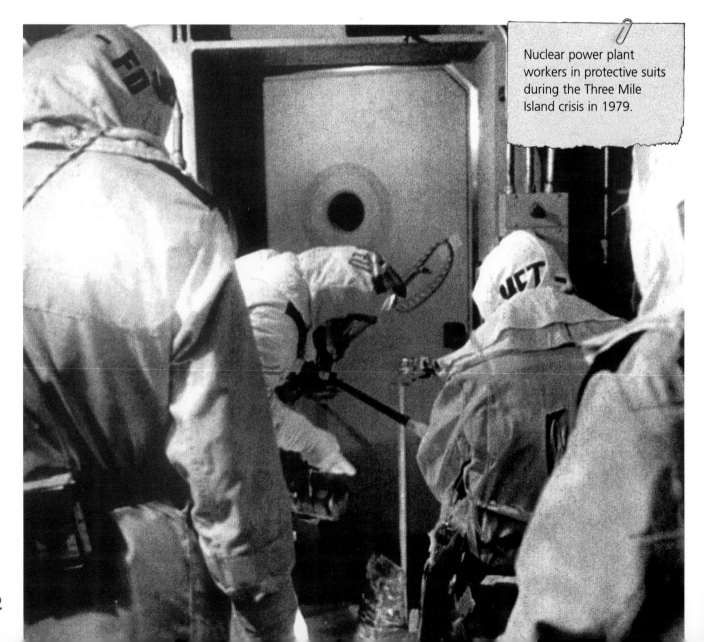

Nuclear power plant workers in protective suits during the Three Mile Island crisis in 1979.

Over the years, accidental leakages of radiation from nuclear power plants have poisoned the land nearby. This photo shows contaminated land in Siberia.

Without water the reactor began to overheat and disintegrate. One consequence of this was the formation of a highly inflammable bubble of hydrogen and oxygen gas inside the reactor. If the reactor had disintegrated and the gas had exploded, a disaster of Chernobyl-like proportions would have occurred. It has been estimated that Three Mile Island was just twenty seconds away from such a major explosion, and only an emergency reactor core cooling system saved the plant.

In the Soviet Union, disasters were more spectacular. In 1957, an accident at a remote nuclear fuel reprocessing plant near Chelyabinsk released radiation over a large area, which had to be evacuated and sealed off. Among other incidents, in 1978 the Byeloyarsk reactor went out of control after a fire and, in 1982, the No. 1 reactor at Chernobyl was severely damaged as a result of operational errors. Worst of all, in 1985, incompetent procedures resulted in 14 people being scalded to death by super-heated steam during the start-up procedure at Balakovo power station.

The Chelyabinsk Disaster

" As far as I could see, it was empty land…no villages, no towns, only chimneys of destroyed homes….It was like the moon for many hundreds of square kilometers, useless and unproductive for a very long time. "

Soviet scientist Lev Tumerman on driving through Chelyabinsk in 1960. Quoted in The Nuclear Barons *by Peter Pringle and James Spigelman.*

In the Soviet Union especially, accidents caused by poor training, machine faults, and flawed reactors all went unreported to other nuclear power workers. No one had the opportunity to learn from the mistakes of others, and an atmosphere of complacency was allowed to develop.

Stalin (second left), surrounded by senior Communist Party colleagues, in Moscow's Red Square in 1935.

IN 1900 RUSSIA WAS A vast, sprawling monarchy, and outside of a few major cities its people lived in rural poverty. During World War I, the monarchy was overthrown by a communist revolution and Russia was renamed the Soviet Union. During the 1920s and 1930s, the communists turned their backward country into a modern, industrial nation.

Under the command of Soviet leader Joseph Stalin, factories, hydroelectric dams, and steel works were built with extraordinary speed.

Then, in 1941, Nazi Germany invaded, with the intention of turning the Soviet Union into a German colony and its population into slaves. A combination

A parade in Moscow celebrates the military strength of the Soviet Union.

of Soviet soldiers fighting with great courage and tanks, guns, and airplanes from the new factories drove out the invaders. World War II transformed the Soviet Union and the United States into the world's two superpowers. But when the war ended in 1945, rivalry between these superpowers led to an armed standoff known as "The Cold War," which was made all the more dangerous by the development of new nuclear weapons.

By the 1960s, under the leadership of Leonid Brezhnev, the Soviet Union entered an era that became known as "the period of stagnation." Its leaders were cut off from the realities of life, and protected from criticism by a combination of obsessive secrecy and a secret police force that arrested and imprisoned any critic of the government's damaging policies. The Soviet Union's economy was run by ministries that jealously competed against each other for the control of resources. The authoritarian government stifled initiative and taught its citizens to have complete faith in the Communist Party.

It was during this time that the nuclear power plant at Chernobyl was built and began operation. It was staffed by managers and workers who believed the myth that Soviet reactors were totally safe. But along with this misplaced faith in their technology, there was also a general apathy and lack of responsibility. This attitude afflicted all of Soviet industry and seems to

have been a reaction to a culture that treated any kind of criticism of Communist Party policy as a form of treason.

Mikhail Gorbachev (1931–)

In 1985 the Soviet Union came under the control of Mikhail Gorbachev. Although a dedicated communist, Gorbachev admitted that there were terrible things wrong with the Soviet system. He spoke of "a spirit of servility, fawning, clannishness, and persecution of independent thinkers...and personal and clan ties between leaders." His remedy was a combination of *glasnost*, meaning greater openness and honesty, and *perestroika*, meaning reform and restructuring of his country's economy and political system.

Although much admired in the West, Gorbachev was deeply unpopular among many of his Communist Party colleagues, who resented their loss of power and influence. In 1991 there was an attempted *coup* against him. He resigned and was replaced as president by Boris Yeltsin, who oversaw the dissolution of the Soviet Union into Russia and a number of independent states.

DURING THE 1970s AND early 1980s, the Soviet Union carried out a widespread reactor building program. It was a time when nuclear fuel seemed to be cheaper than the more traditional oil and coal. "Nuclear power plants are like stars that shine all day long,' declared one senior Soviet scientist, M. A. Styrikovich. "We shall sow them all over the land. They are perfectly safe!"

Work on the Chernobyl plant began in 1972. Reactors were of the thermal type (see pages 8–9) and of a Russian design known as the RBMK. These reactors had already gained a questionable reputation among some Soviet scientists because they leaked dangerously high amounts of radiation. Still, in the climate of the time, no one dared challenge the decision to install them at Chernobyl. The plant itself consisted of four reactors, with plans for two more to be built. Constructed 68 miles (110 km) north of the Ukrainian capital of Kiev (the third largest city in the Soviet Union), it was serviced by workers who lived in the nearby towns of Chernobyl and Pripyat.

A staff recruitment advertisement published before the disaster—"Wanted: Operators for Nuclear Power Plant in the Ukraine. No experience necessary…"— speaks volumes for the lax attitude toward training and safety that prevailed both at the plant and in the Soviet nuclear industry.

In the years before the explosion, Soviet physicist Grigori Medvedev wrote several articles questioning the safety of Russian reactors, but he could not find a publisher. One rejected his work, saying, "What do you mean? Academicians [scientists] are always writing that Soviet nuclear power plants are

ЧОРНОБИЛЬСЬКА АЕС ІМЕНІ В. І. ЛЕНІНА

This statue of revolutionary leader Lenin outside Chernobyl Power Plant was intended to make the link between communism and progress clear to all.

perfectly safe....In the West this kind of thing could happen, but not here!"

Not everyone, though, was quite so blind to the danger. In 1985 A. P. Aleksandrov, a senior Soviet scientist, commented to colleagues, "Fate has been kind to us, comrades, in that we haven't had a Pennsylvania (Three Mile Island) of our own."

Within a year, fate was to take a terrible turn for the worse....

Nikolai Fomin (1937–)

In 1972 the chief engineer at Chernobyl, Nikolai Fomin, arrived to work on its construction. Fomin was very proud of his nuclear reactor, and would assure visitors that the chances of a disaster there were about the same as being hit by a comet. His training was in electrical engineering rather than nuclear energy, but he frequently said that this was not a problem since running a reactor was such a simple job. In late 1985 he suffered serious spinal injuries in a car crash. He returned to work only a month before the disaster. The pain he still felt from his injuries no doubt affected his judgment in the crucial moments leading up to the explosion at Chernobyl.

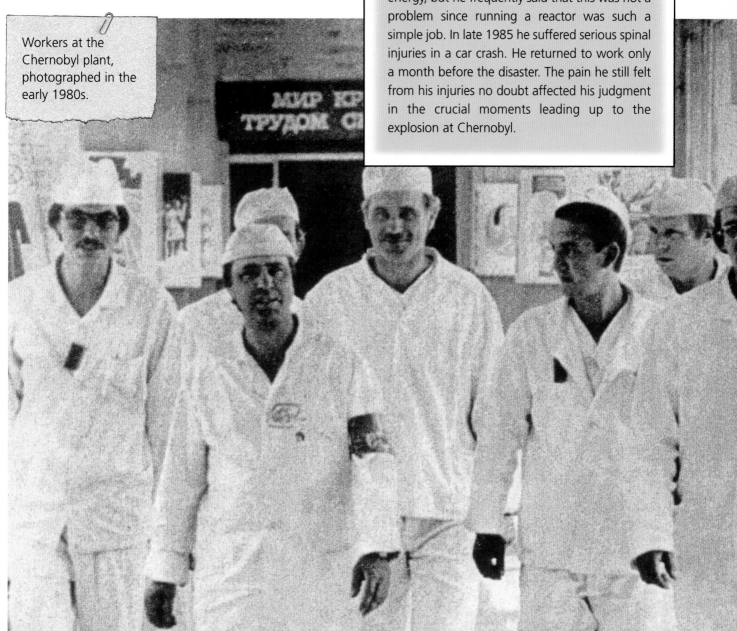

Workers at the Chernobyl plant, photographed in the early 1980s.

Workers take the bus to another shift at the Chernobyl Power Plant a few weeks before the explosion.

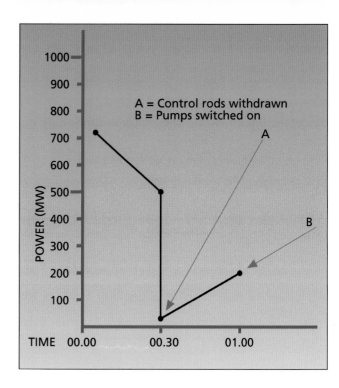

A = Control rods withdrawn
B = Pumps switched on

APRIL 25

11:10 P.M. The staff at the Chernobyl plant received permission from the electricity controller for Kiev to proceed with their test and continue with the shutdown of the reactor. Overseeing the experiment was the power plant's deputy chief engineer, Anatoli Dyatlov.

APRIL 26

12:00 Midnight The night shift began, but some of the staff from the afternoon shift decided to remain in the control room to watch the emergency electrical power test. Shift foreman Alexander Akimov and senior reactor engineer Leonid Toptunov took over the controls of the reactor. After examining the situation, they felt the power in the reactor had already been reduced to too low a level to proceed with the test, but Dyatlov insisted they continue.

12:05 A.M. The power level of the reactor continued to be reduced and at this point registered 720 MW (megawatts)—way below its usual operational level of 3,000 MW. No one in the control room really understood the extreme danger of this procedure—that a flaw in the RBMK reactor design made it incredibly unstable at low power. The reactor soon began to behave in an unpredictable and highly volatile way. Anatoli Dyatlov's response to the baffling readings shown by instruments in the control room was to shout and swear at his staff, blaming their incompetence for the reactor's behavior.

12:30 A.M. Power dropped to 500 MW, then to an unexpected 30 MW. This huge drop led the operators to withdraw a number of control rods in order to bring the reactor back to a safer operational level. This was the moment at which the experiment should have been stopped, but Dyatlov grew impatient and insisted that his staff go ahead.

01:00 A.M. To stabilize the reactor, power was increased, and it climbed to 200 MW. Pumps were switched on to increase the flow of cooling water to the core. But switching on the pumps reduced the water levels in other parts of the reactor and, like an almost empty kettle, it began to boil dry.

Although the reactor was now becoming ominously unstable, the disaster was still not inevitable. Dyatlov could have realized that the situation was too dangerous to continue the test, and the emergency core cooling system could have been switched back on and the reactor completely shut down.

A Moment in Time

At 12:30 A.M., as power falls to 30 MW, a 26-year-old reactor operator, Leonid Toptunov, begins to argue with Anatoli Dyatlov in the control room of the Chernobyl No. 4 reactor. He questions the wisdom of increasing power, instead of closing the reactor down as his training has instructed him to do. Dyatlov, who has already created a tense and unpleasant atmosphere in the control room, becomes enraged by his young subordinate's impertinence, and threatens to replace him with another worker if he does not do as he is ordered.

From control panels such as this, Chernobyl's technicians set in motion the world's worst nuclear accident.

19

01:20 A.M. Following the panic and ill-feeling of the previous hour, the control room staff settled down and an atmosphere of normality returned. Even Dyatlov had calmed down and seemed confident about the forthcoming test. Only Akimov and Toptunov remained concerned about their instructions and were convinced that the reactor should be shut down. They were right to be worried. In their attempts to get the reactor to settle at a lower power level, the control room staff had made it extremely unstable. Just as the reactor began to reach a critical, overheated condition, and the cooling water at the core started to turn to superheated steam, Dyatlov ordered his test to go ahead.

01:22 A.M. As the water flow decreased, steam began to be generated at the reactor core.

01:23 A.M. The test was started. Steam from the reactor to the turbine was shut off. The turbine continued to rotate under its own huge momentum, but as it slowed, it generated less electricity and the pumps provided less and less vital cooling water for the reactor core.

01:23:21 A.M. As the reactor continued to overheat, steam generated inside the core increased uncontrollably. At the end of a long

A reactor hall at Chernobyl identical to the one that was the site of the disaster. The reactor lies beneath the tiled, circular feature at the bottom of the photograph. The huge mechanism in the background is a refueling machine for the reactor.

corridor 328 feet (100 m) away from the reactor, staff in the control room heard a series of ominous thumps that made the ground tremble beneath their feet.

01:23:40 A.M. Akimov noticed a massive power increase in the reactor and pressed the emergency button on his console, designed to send control rods into the reactor core to shut it down. At that moment, shift foreman Valeri Perevozchenko rushed in from the reactor hall with the alarming news that the heavy steel covers on the reactor access points were jumping up and down in their sockets.

01:23:44 A.M. As the control rods descended, the reactor power increased to more than 100 times its safety limit. At this moment, the rods jammed. Their path along the channels down to the core had been buckled and distorted by the already disintegrating reactor.

01:23:45 A.M. Fuel pellets in the fuel rods inside the reactor core started to shatter, turning the cooling water to hydrogen and oxygen and producing a pulse of high pressure in the fuel channels.

A Moment in Time

At 01:23 A.M., as the power levels continue to rise, instruments in the control room indicate that the reactor is boiling dry, despite attempts to get more cooling water into the core. Akimov is angry and confused, and Toptunov is white with fear. Dyatlov looks totally confused. The ground trembles beneath their feet. No one really understands why the immensely powerful reactor is running completely out of control.

Chernobyl technicians tend to a refueling machine inside a reactor hall in the days before the incident.

I T WAS FORTUNATE FOR MANY of the technicians in
the No. 4 reactor control room that there was a
significant distance between them and the reactor
hall. If they had been any closer, they might all have
been killed in the initial blast. Yet for some this would
have been a mercy, because they were fated to die
agonizing, drawn-out deaths over the days and
weeks to come.

When the explosion occurred at 1:24 A.M. it was truly
colossal. The walls of the control room
shook, the ceiling cracked open, and
all the lights went out. Then, as
doors were blown open,

dust and smoke billowed in from the connecting
corridor and covered much of the room in a thin, gray
film. Immediately a sharp, distinct smell filled the
control room. Everyone there recalled it being like air
after a thunderstorm, only a great deal stronger.

The explosion destroyed the reactor with such force
that a 60-ton concrete shield was thrown into the air
and now lay to one side. Known as the "biological
shield," it had been built above the core to protect
plant workers from radiation. A massive
machine that was used to supply the
reactor with nuclear fuel had
collapsed on top of it.

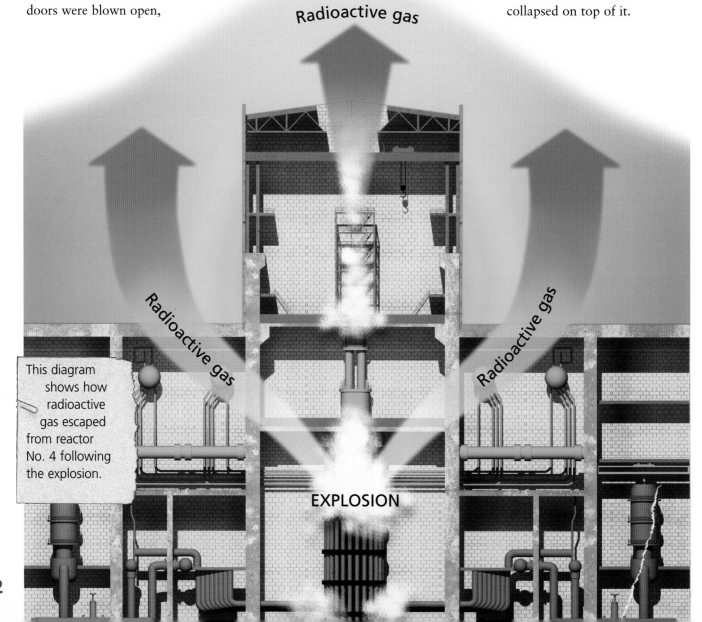

Radioactive gas

Radioactive gas

Radioactive gas

This diagram
shows how
radioactive
gas escaped
from reactor
No. 4 following
the explosion.

EXPLOSION

The ruins of the Chernobyl power plant, photographed three days after its explosion.

A Catastrophe in Tons

The Chernobyl explosion unleashed

- 55 tons of nuclear fuel into the atmosphere in the form of smoke and ash;
- 77 tons of nuclear fuel and 770 tons of radioactive graphite into the immediate vicinity of the power plant.

The exposed and blazing reactor core also contained a further

- 55 tons of nuclear fuel;
- 880 tons of reactor graphite.

The contents of the reactor—uranium fuel and highly radioactive graphite—now lay exposed in the disintegrated core and scattered around the hall. Steam from the cooling water was also escaping into the hall and the surrounding atmosphere. In other parts of the world, nuclear reactors were built with a concrete outer shell to contain radiation leaks. Unfortunately, the Chernobyl reactor, along with many other Soviet reactors, lacked this now-essential safety feature. The explosion had blown a hole in the high hall ceiling, and red-hot graphite hurled up by the blast had set the asphalt roof on fire.

Sadly, the dazed technicians inside the control room did not understand that their reactor was no more, nor that its remains were exposed to the outside world and spewing out lethal radiation. If Anatoli Dyatlov and his staff had realized this, then perhaps more lives would have been saved in the immediate aftermath of the disaster.

23

IMMEDIATELY FOLLOWING THE EXPLOSION, foreman Valeri Perevozchenko thought not of himself but of his colleague, Valera Khodemchuck, whom he had last seen in the towering reactor hall. Perevozchenko dashed there, but his progress was slowed by clouds of dust and blazing rubble. The nearer he drew to the hall, the stranger and more nightmarish his world became. The air seemed very thick; he was aware of a sinister burning sensation in his throat, lungs, and eyes. The taste of sour apples lay heavy in his mouth. Perevozchenko realized that his body was absorbing massive amounts of lethal radiation. He told himself not to panic, and ran on across floors that cracked with broken glass.

When he reached the reactor hall, Perevozchenko discovered a mass of tangled wreckage and a hole in the roof. Little waterfalls poured from shattered pipes and splattered on to the floor. Small fires cast dark shadows among the mangled machinery. Firemen had already arrived on the roof, and their shouts echoed around the huge hall, mingling with the moaning sound of burning graphite from the reactor core.

Perevozchenko stood next to this hellish scene. He could not see much in the dark, but already the radiation was turning his skin brown—giving him a so-called "nuclear tan." He called out for his friend, and when there was no reply he began to tear with

The turbine hall contained highly inflammable fuel, but was saved from destruction by the heroism of plant workers.

his bare hands at a pile of rubble where he thought Khodemchuck might be. Exhausted and feeling nauseous from the huge dose of lethal radiation he had received, Perevozchenko returned to the control room. On his way back he noticed that the reactor cover had been completely blown off. Back in the control room he struggled to explain this to Akimov. But neither Akimov nor Dyatlov was prepared to believe him. Akimov was convinced that the reactor was still intact and, along with other colleagues, went to the hall to turn valves that would send water to cool it down. As they laboriously turned the valve wheels, they too were exposed to lethal radiation. Their bodies turned brown, and they fell into a fever and, eventually, a coma.

Elsewhere, other power plant workers had greater success. Staff in the turbine room next to the reactor quickly drained away highly inflammable fuels from storage tanks. Four of them would also die from the effects of radiation in the weeks to come, but they saved the plant from even greater catastrophe.

A Moment in Time

In the control room at 1:30 A.M., foreman Alexander Akimov turns to Victor Proskuryakov and Alexander Kudryavtsev and tells them: "The control rods have jammed. Run to the reactor and lower them by hand...." The two men run off through the debris and peer into the mouth of the open reactor. They return, both fatally exposed, to report that the reactor has been destroyed. Dyatlov dismisses their observations, insisting that the reactor is still intact.

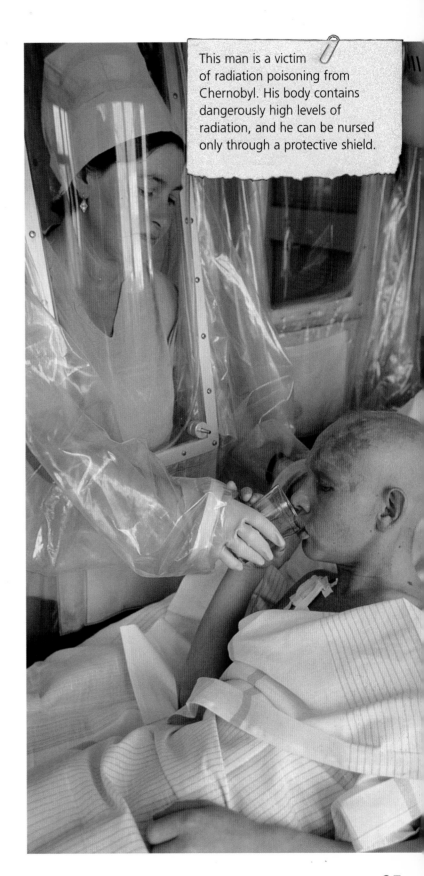

This man is a victim of radiation poisoning from Chernobyl. His body contains dangerously high levels of radiation, and he can be nursed only through a protective shield.

IMMEDIATELY FOLLOWING THE EXPLOSION, the alarm bell sounded at the fire station just 1,640 feet (500 m) away from the No. 4 reactor. It was the fate of No. 2 fire patrol, under the command of Lieutenant Vladimir Pravik, to be on duty that night. They raced at once to the stricken reactor and within minutes were on the collapsing roof, attempting to control the fire there and pouring water down onto the blaze below.

Through gaps in the roof they could see the ruptured reactor beneath them. It looked like the cauldron of a volcano, and was pouring out lethal radiation at a fantastic rate. Pravik's fire crew could sense these deadly rays clawing at them and they began to feel unbearably hot, both inside and outside their bodies. They were not only being poisoned by radiation. The tar that lined the roof was melting, releasing dense toxic smoke, and sticking to their boots as they moved. The roof was likely to collapse at any moment. All too soon, the men began to feel sick, but every one of them kept on fighting the fires that surrounded them.

Soon afterward the fire station commander, Major Leonid Telyatnikov, arrived. He had been celebrating his birthday, but rushed to the fire as soon as he heard what was happening. Telyatnikov understood at once that the power

These salvage workers are wearing protective gear that was unavailable to the firefighters who first arrived on the scene.

plant was facing a major catastrophe, and he gave orders that every available fire crew in the area be summoned at once.

He told his men to stand at their posts and fight the fire until it had been extinguished, and they did so with extraordinary heroism. But raw courage was not enough. Many men, fainting and vomiting, could not continue, so others rushed to fill their place. Through their extraordinary efforts, the fires started by the reactor explosion did not spread to the rest of the plant. By daybreak their work was done, but they had paid a terrible price for their efforts. Later that day, 17 firemen were airlifted to a specialist hospital in Moscow to be treated for severe radiation poisoning. During the next few weeks, all of them would die agonizing deaths.

A Widow's Tale

“ The last two days in the hospital, I would lift his arm, and the bone would rattle loose, the flesh had separated from it. He coughed up pieces of lung and liver. He was choking on his insides....It's impossible to tell this! It shouldn't be written.... ”

Ludmila Ignatenko, widow of firefighter Vasily Ignatenko, from Voices from Chernobyl *by Svetlana Alexievich.*

Once the fire was extinguished, tons of radioactive debris had to be cleared away. These workers are on the roof of the reactor hall.

By DAWN THE FIRES ON the roof of No. 4 reactor had been extinguished and there was now little danger of the blaze spreading to other parts of the power plant. But inside, the open reactor would continue to burn for another nine days. In normal conditions, the maximum permissible radiation dose for a nuclear power plant worker is five roentgens a year. In the days after the accident at Chernobyl, the radiation level fluctuated from between 1,000 to 20,000 roentgens *an hour*.

On the morning of April 26, power plant director Victor Brukhanov and chief engineer Nikolai Fomin met to assess the damage. They sent the following message to their superiors in Moscow and Kiev: "The reactor is intact. We are supplying water to it. There was an explosion in the emergency water tank in the central hall. The radiation situation is within normal limits. One man has been killed...." How they could have gotten it so wrong is a mystery. Perhaps they could not bring themselves to believe such a catastrophe had overtaken them. They were not alone. In the hours following the disaster, Chernobyl's beleaguered workers continued to try to supply more cooling water to a reactor that had already been destroyed. The ruptured water pipes leading into the inferno simply flooded the electrical equipment on the lower floors of the reactor building.

This photograph, taken from a helicopter immediately after the fire had been extinguished, shows the damage the explosion inflicted on the No. 4 reactor hall.

Shock and Disbelief

"It's a strange thing, but during those truly weird hours [after the explosion], the overwhelming majority of the operational staff, including me, believed what they wanted to believe and not what was really happening. "

Viktor Smagin, shift foreman, No. 4 unit.

The misunderstanding of the scale of the disaster was especially tragic for the inhabitants of nearby Chernobyl town and Pripyat. In an accident such as this, people should be instructed to close their windows and stay indoors. Instead, no warnings were given. Children still trotted out to play in the streets. Mothers flocked to the market to shop. They may have heard rumors about an accident at the plant, but no one was able or allowed to tell them how much danger they were putting themselves in, basking in the fallout on that fine, Saturday morning in late spring.

As workers erect a protective concrete case around the ruined reactor, a technician tests for radiation levels.

A Moment in Time

Late on the afternoon of April 26 at the Chernobyl power plant, Dr. Valentin Belokon moves among the casualties of the accident, administering antiradiation drugs and painkillers. He tries to comfort the severely injured men, some of whom are hysterical with fear and pain. He was working the night shift at Pripyat hospital when he heard about the accident, and he rushed at once to the scene. Belokon has now been administering emergency aid for almost 24 hours solid, and is beginning to suffer the headaches and nausea that are sure symptoms of radiation sickness. He stumbles, retching and gasping for breath. A colleague tells him to go home and rest, but Belokon refuses. "When people see a man in a white coat, it makes them quieter," he reasons. He stays on the site until the next day, by which time he is too weak to continue working.

THERE WERE TWO OBVIOUS and separate causes of the Chernobyl disaster. One of them was the reactor itself; the other was the people who operated it. The RBMK reactor was a flawed design, which was unstable at low power and had no concrete containment building around it. The operators were poorly trained and, because they had no proper understanding of the reactor, made serious mistakes when problems began to occur.

However, there was another, less obvious, major cause of the accident—and this was the Soviet system of government and the society it produced. The Soviet Union was so determined to protect its regime, and the communist philosophy upon which it was based, that it severely punished its critics. So-called "dissidents" (Russian people who dared to criticize and protest their country's faults) were often dismissed as mentally ill, or sent to prison camps in the most bleak and uncomfortable regions. An atmosphere of obsessive secrecy surrounded anything to do with the Soviet "national interest." Nuclear power, and its close links with nuclear weapons, was an especially sensitive topic.

The Perils of Criticism

" That young writer Medvedev, who has been writing such garbage about us, might find himself taken some place far, far away, so that by the time he comes back, if he ever does, he will be bald and gray, and not at all young. "

Threatening words from senior Soviet minister Sokolov, directed at Grigori Medvedev, scientist, writer, and critic of the Soviet nuclear industry in the early 1980s, quoted in Medvedev's book No Breathing Room—The Aftermath of Chernobyl.

Shortly after the disaster a scientist removes a dead fish from the lake next to the plant, which can be seen in the top right of this photograph.

This attitude led to an alarming atmosphere of complacency in the Soviet nuclear industry, exaggerated by the fact that accidents and breakdowns at other nuclear plants were kept secret. News of such events was withheld even from workers within the industry, so valuable lessons were never learned. The workers at Chernobyl had been told that the plant, and nuclear power, were perfectly safe. They did not treat their potentially dangerous reactor with the caution it deserved and became careless. Just before his death from radiation poisoning on May 11, 1986, shift foreman Alexander Akimov kept repeating over and over, "I did everything right. I don't understand why it happened." Bewildered and humiliated, he was a victim of the poor training and lack of understanding that had infected the whole Soviet nuclear industry.

By Western standards, the attitude of the Soviet government toward its ordinary citizens was uncommonly callous. Perhaps the hardship of the revolution, forced industrialization, and World War II had produced a generation of government officials who had little sympathy for the lives and trials of ordinary people. At a Moscow press conference two weeks after the disaster, one senior Soviet politician, A. M. Petrosyants, declared in defense of his country's nuclear industry, "Science requires victims."

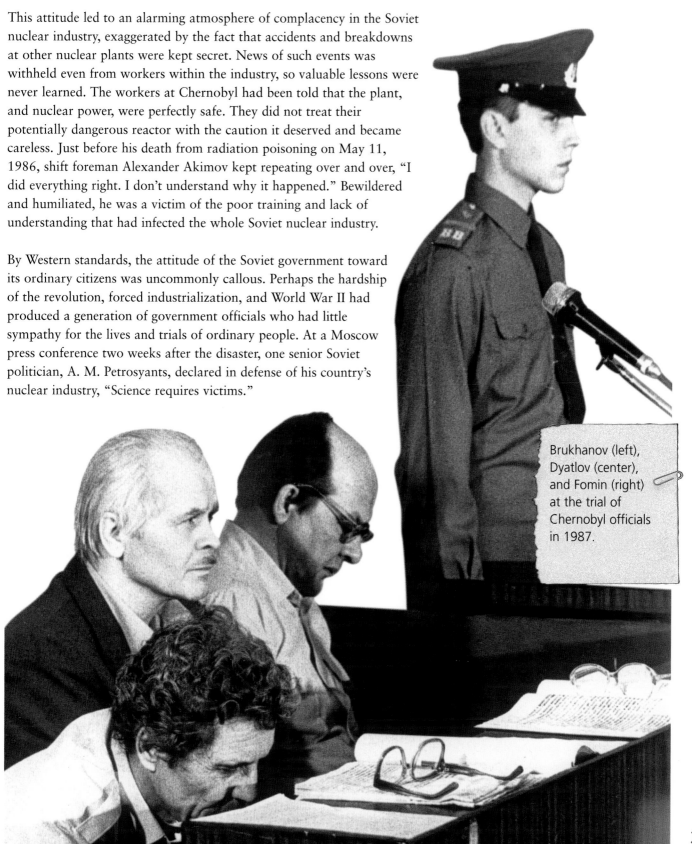

Brukhanov (left), Dyatlov (center), and Fomin (right) at the trial of Chernobyl officials in 1987.

In the days after the explosion, helicopters flew over the plant to drop sand, boron, and other materials onto the open reactor.

A Moment in Time

It is just another Monday morning on April 28, 1986, in the streets of Chernobyl. But Mikhail Byckau, a nuclear scientist, realizes that there has been an accident and tries to warn people to go indoors. He approaches a street vendor, and tells her to stop selling sausages because radioactive rain is falling. She does not believe him and tells him, "If there had been an accident, they'd have announced it on radio and TV."

IN THE SOVIET UNION it was official policy for any information about nuclear accidents to remain top secret. In the immediate aftermath of the Chernobyl disaster, radiation levels in the area were dangerously high. But Soviet state secrecy meant that many people in the Ukraine and the neighboring region of Belorussia (now Belarus) were needlessly exposed to radioactivity. One nuclear scientist at the nearby Belorussia Academy of Sciences arrived at work on Monday morning to find his radiation detection equipment going haywire. He and his colleagues quickly realized that there had been an accident at the Chernobyl power plant. They called friends, warning them to stay indoors. But around midday the phones were cut off—no doubt in an attempt by the Soviet authorities to stop the news from breaking out.

However, a story of such magnitude could not be kept quiet for long. On April 28, the Soviet news agency TASS issued a terse two-line statement about the accident. By April 30, the news had been carried in most Soviet papers. But on May 1, in nearby Kiev, the traditional May Day parade still took place.

This was not so remarkable, because the Soviet people had been told that what had happened was only a minor problem.

The first priority was to cover up the reactor to stop any further leaking of lethal radiation. The most practical and safest way to do this was to use helicopters to drop sand, boron, dolomite, clay, and lead on top of it. More than 5,500 tons of this material were dropped to extinguish the blaze and cover the reactor.

Soldiers, many fresh from the Soviet war in Afghanistan, were drafted in to help with the cleanup. More than 600,000 of these workers, known as "liquidators," were used. It is impossible to say to what degree their health suffered—partly because the effects of their exposure to radiation may only become evident in cancers that will form in later life.

Once this initial task had been completed, it was then judged safe enough to build a huge cover over the reactor. By December 1986, a 330,000-ton concrete casing had been constructed. It was named the "sarcophagus," a Latin word meaning tomb, for within it lay the remains of Valera Khodemchuck—the only casualty of the accident whose body had never been recovered.

Workers, wearing alarmingly little protective clothing, pose for press photographers with a banner proclaiming: "We shall fulfill the government's goal."

The huge concrete sarcophagus built over the No. 4 reactor was completed a year after the explosion.

With no realistic assessment of the health risks caused by the Chernobyl accident, the traditional May Day parade in nearby Kiev still went ahead.

THE REST OF THE world found out about the extent of the Chernobyl accident very shortly after April 26, when scientists in Sweden, and then the rest of Europe, began to pick up abnormally high radiation readings. A "radiation plume" carried by high winds spread all the way from Chernobyl through to the Mediterranean, northern Europe, and as far west as Wales and Iceland. To the east, traces of radiation were detected across Russia from Chernobyl to the Pacific, through Japan, and even as far as the west coast of the United States. What Chernobyl showed all too graphically was that, as far as nuclear accidents were concerned, the world was really quite a small place.

The early days following the Chernobyl disaster were influenced by the Cold War politics of the day. In the 1980s, the Soviet Union was a deadly and suspicious rival of the West (meaning mainly Western Europe and the United States). This rivalry was reflected in the defensive language used by President Gorbachev when he spoke to his country in a broadcast four months after the disaster. Gorbachev began by making the

point that the United States also had its technological disasters, referring to the tragic explosion of the *Challenger* space shuttle earlier in 1986. He said, "The loss of the *Challenger* crew and the accident at the Chernobyl nuclear power station have heightened our sense of alarm and been a cruel reminder that

Gorbachev Speaks to His People

" Good evening, comrades. All of you know that there has been a terrible misfortune—the accident at the Chernobyl nuclear power plant. It has painfully affected the Soviet people, and shocked the international community. For the first time, we confront the real force of nuclear energy out of control. "

National television broadcast to the Soviet people, 1986.

mankind is still trying to come to grips with the fantastic, powerful forces which it has itself brought into being...."

The initial secrecy of the Soviets meant that, in the West, the story got out of hand. Western tabloid newspapers (especially the more lurid ones) were desperate for information, and made sensational and misleading headlines from any rumor or scrap of news they heard. Some newspapers painted a picture of Belorussia and Ukraine cloaked in lethal radiation —and portrayed a desolate land where soldiers in ABC suits were burying hundreds of thousands of citizens in huge pits. At one press conference in New York, a Soviet scientist was surrounded by journalists frantic to know how many people had died. "Give us a number, any number," shouted one newspaper man, desperate for a story.

Gradually, Gorbachev's new policy of *glasnost* was applied to Chernobyl, and a fuller picture began to emerge, for both the citizens of the Soviet Union and the rest of the world. The story was a tragic one, but not quite in the way that had been imagined at the time.

This map shows the 18-mile (30-km) contamination zone that was declared around Chernobyl.

The yellow shading on this map shows how far the radioactive cloud from Chernobyl had spread by May 6, 1986.

The cleanup operation in full swing. These army vehicles are spraying roads near the Chernobyl plant, a couple of weeks after the explosion.

At 11:00 A.M. on the day following the explosion, the citizens of Pripyat have their Sunday morning disturbed by the following loudspeaker announcement: "Attention. Attention. Honorable comrades! Following an accident at the Chernobyl nuclear power plant, an unfavorable radiation situation is arising in the town....Today...beginning at 1400 hours [2:00 P.M.], it will be necessary to start a temporary evacuation of the town's inhabitants...."

O NCE IT BECAME APPARENT that the No. 4 reactor had indeed been destroyed and that radiation was pouring out of the power station and contaminating the surrounding countryside, the Soviet authorities decided they had to act to protect the local people. One-and-a-half days after the explosion, the evacuation of Pripyat and Chernobyl began. Residents lined up for transportation bound for the south and temporary accommodation in the Kiev region. Hundreds of buses arrived, and 50,000 people, including 17,000 children, were whisked away. They were told they would be back in a few days. Many people were distressed at having to leave their pets behind. The evacuation of animals was strictly forbidden, as it was known that radiation collected in dangerously high levels in feathers and fur.

Most of the citizens of Chernobyl and Pripyat never did return to their homes. The pavements and squares of their once proud towns would soon be covered with weeds, and their schools, office buildings, and homes would fall into disrepair. The pets they left behind met a grim fate. With no one to feed them, the dogs reverted to their wild state, gathered into

Residents of a village near Chernobyl gather up valuables and necessities. Many of those who left would never return.

Once a thriving community, Pripyat became a ghost town almost overnight.

Notes Left on the Doors of Abandoned Houses

" *Dear friend, don't bother looking for expensive things. We don't have any. Use whatever you need, but don't loot. We'll be back.* "

" *Forgive us, our house!* "

In a child's writing: " *Don't kill our Zhulka. She's a good dog.* "

Quoted in Voices from Chernobyl.

" *All around people were saying, we're going to die, we're going to die....My daughter was 6 years old. I was putting her to bed and she whispered in my ear, 'Papa, I want to live. I'm still little.'* "

The words of a Pripyat resident.

Evacuees from the Chernobyl region are monitored for radiation contamination.

packs, and hunted down the cats. They in turn were shot by soldiers who came to the town. Many of the soldiers, although hardened war veterans, found the process of shooting people's pets and other local wildlife quite upsetting.

As radiation had fallen across thousands of square miles of Ukraine and nearby Belorussia, a huge cleanup operation began. Topsoil, vegetation, trees, and dead animals all had to be buried, and even buildings and roads were cleaned to try to remove the lethal contamination of the accident.

This computer simulation shows how radioactive contamination spread east and west from Chernobyl across the northern hemisphere.

THE COST OF THE CHERNOBYL accident to the Soviet Union was quite possibly too much to bear. Decades of communism, especially during "the years of stagnation," had left a huge country ill-equipped to cope with such a disaster. Aside from the direct human suffering caused by deaths during the accident, there were phenomenal cleanup costs running into billions of rubles, and the financial drain of long-term medical treatment and resettlement costs for the hundreds of thousands of people affected.

The Soviet leadership was slow to acknowledge the accident, but when it did, the frankness with which faults were admitted surprised the world. Nonetheless, the old habits died hard, and when those held responsible for the disaster came to trial they were made scapegoats for the Soviet system as a whole.

Plant director Brukhanov and engineers Fomin and Dyatlov may have acted unwisely, perhaps even foolishly, but they were molded by the system that had produced them, and victims of their own ignorance. Instead of placing some of the blame on the faults of the RBMK reactor (and thus undermining the whole Soviet nuclear industry), the government blamed the disaster on "violations of discipline and regulations guaranteeing safety at plants." All three men and two other senior workers at the plant were sentenced to ten years' imprisonment.

Chernobyl highlighted the failings of the Soviet Union. And, instead of leading its citizens to consider reform of their political system, it resulted in a widespread loss of faith in communism and the conviction that the old order should be swept away. Within five years of the accident, the Soviet Union had collapsed.

The most obvious effect in the rest of the world was to heighten public suspicion of nuclear power (see pages 10–11). But there were more immediate concerns, too. In Poland, millions of children were given medicine to help counter the effects of radiation, and throughout Western Europe huge quantities of milk and vegetables contaminated by radiation had to be destroyed. Because the effects of radiation levels on the human body are difficult to predict, it is currently impossible to say how many people in the world have been affected by the disaster. One estimate suggests that, in the years to come, perhaps an additional 2,500 people worldwide will contract cancers as a result, but other studies suggest the figure will be far higher.

Gorbachev Remembers

" Chernobyl shed light on many of the sicknesses of our system...the concealing or hushing up of accidents and other bad news, irresponsibility and carelessness, slipshod work....The accident...was graphic evidence not only of how obsolete our technology was, but also of the failure of the old system. At the same time, and such is the irony of history, it severely affected our reforms by literally knocking the country off its tracks. "

Memoirs, published in 1995.

Soviet army trucks and other vehicles used in the cleanup operation were too contaminated by radiation to use again. They were abandoned in dumps close to the power plant.

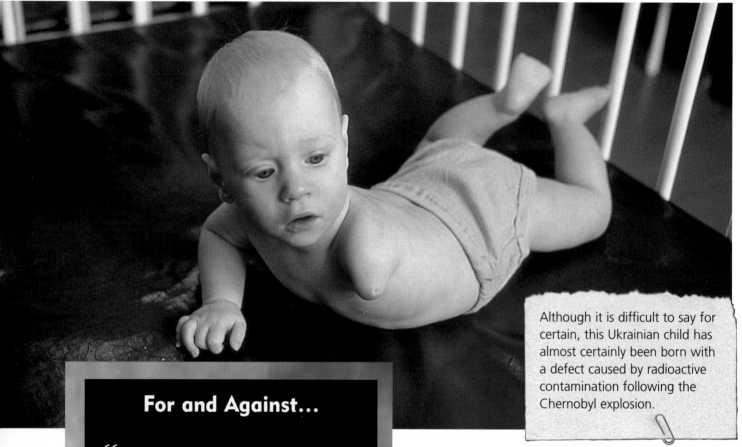

Although it is difficult to say for certain, this Ukrainian child has almost certainly been born with a defect caused by radioactive contamination following the Chernobyl explosion.

For and Against...

" The Chernobyl accident certainly was not an insignificant tragedy. It should not, however, be used to justify the vilification of nuclear power [the belief that nuclear power is worthless]. All energy sources will involve some accidental risks.... "

Nuclear engineer Michael Baker, University of Wisconsin-Madison, quoted in an editorial for the Badger Herald, *an online university newspaper, April 1996.*

" The crumbling Chernobyl sarcophagus stands as a testimony to the collapse of the nuclear dream; it is a symbol of the failure of nuclear power. "

Tobias Muenchmeyer, Greenpeace press release, December 15, 2000.

AS THE MEMORY OF Chernobyl fades into history, there are still more than 400 working reactors in existence, altogether providing an estimated one-fifth of the world's electricity. Opponents of nuclear power point to Chernobyl as the most pressing possible reason to abandon this form of energy. The conservation organization Greenpeace declared: "...although Chernobyl remains the largest civil nuclear disaster, it may not be the last. The world has yet to wean itself off the most dangerous energy source yet devised by humankind: nuclear power." The long-term problems of storing dangerous nuclear waste (which will still be lethally radioactive in 150,000 years) are also frequently cited as another major disadvantage.

The pros and cons of the nuclear debate are complicated. Nuclear power plants are not only expensive to build, they are also very expensive to shut down. (The estimated cost for closing and dismantling Great Britain's 35 nuclear reactors, for example, is about $125 billion. This also holds true for those other countries using nuclear energy.) In the Soviet Union, the Chernobyl accident destroyed the blind faith many people had in the benefits of nuclear power. However, Ukraine still gets 45 percent of its energy from its nuclear power plants, and its ailing economy cannot afford to do without them.

Supporters of nuclear power point to the fact that its benefits—cheap power once nuclear power plants have been built, fewer problems resulting from acid rain, greenhouse gases, and other air pollution—were overlooked in an overreaction to the Chernobyl accident. The United States halted its own nuclear power plant building

program after the Three Mile Island disaster in 1979. And the events in Chernobyl only strengthened the doubts of U.S. government policy-makers. However, in 2002, President George W. Bush gave clear signals of a change of heart, indicating that the United States was ready to resume the construction of such power sources to meet the country's growing energy needs.

The accident at Chernobyl has unquestionably had positive effects on the nuclear industry. It was a turning point in the policy of *glasnost*, and safety measures and procedures in Soviet reactors improved rapidly. Today, there is a greater willingness to exchange ideas with European and U.S. scientists. Nuclear power workers in Russia, Ukraine, and other states of the former Soviet Union regularly visit, and are visited by, colleagues from Western nations—a situation impossible to imagine back in 1986.

Children with radiation-related disabilities at a recent demonstration in Kiev for greater financial assistance for the victims of Chernobyl.

BILLIONS OF RUBLES AND millions of dollars of U.S. and European aid have been spent on Chernobyl and the contaminated regions of Ukraine and Belarus. The power plant is now closed, but it remains a major cause for concern. Some scientists think the sarcophagus that surrounds the No. 4 reactor may collapse at any moment, especially in the event of an earthquake.

The final casualty figure for the accident remains as elusive as ever. In Ukraine and Belarus, the social security system operated by the former communist regime has collapsed, but anyone who is able to claim that a disability or debilitating illness is linked to Chernobyl still qualifies for compensation. This tendency to blame illhealth on the disaster regardless of any genuine link makes a clear picture of Chernobyl's real casualties almost impossible to estimate. There are a variety of numbers given for the dead. These figures (particularly those in the hundreds of thousands) are undoubtedly exaggerated—especially by Ukrainian politicians anxious to claim as much aid as they can for their poor, newly independent country. Yet the official number of dead is 32, which is almost certainly too low.

Farmland in the Ukraine and Belarus has been devastated, but farmers are being encouraged to grow oilseed rape. Unlike the traditional grain crops usually grown in this region, rape, also known as canola, does not store radiation in its seeds, which can be used to make lubricants, cooking oil, and animal feed.

Altogether, approximately seven million people have been affected by the accident. The birthrate among local residents has dropped noticeably as a result of anxieties about radiation-related deformities in children. An estimated 2,000 children have become ill with thyroid cancer, and incidents of leukemia have risen slightly. But poorly kept or nonexistent medical records before the disaster make the increases in radiation-linked illnesses very difficult to calculate.

Today the power plant at Chernobyl has closed down, but scientists still regularly monitor radiation levels around the crumbling "sarcophagus."

An abandoned home in a village near the Chernobyl power plant.

Besides, many of these illnesses will only make themselves known in the decades to come. If in ten or twenty years' time a noticeably higher number of people begin to die in their 60s rather than 70s, then perhaps scientists will be able to say with greater certainty that Chernobyl is the cause.

In the catalog of human suffering brought about by Chernobyl, there is one indisputable certainty—the terrible hardship suffered by those who had to leave their homes. Shortly after the accident 170,000 people were evacuated, and another 210,000 were moved out later. This huge upheaval created its own massive problems, and many scientists now believe that the illnesses (both mental and physical) affecting Chernobyl's displaced victims have been caused by this, rather than the effects of radiation. Today, some of the region's residents have returned to the Chernobyl area and live among the decaying houses, eating food grown in contaminated soil. What fate awaits them, only time will tell.

Chernobyl Memories

"Those of us who were there get together on April 26....They could not have managed without us. Our system, a military one, works very well in emergencies...at such moments, Russians can show how great they are! Unique! We'll never become Dutch or German...we'll never have long-lasting asphalt or neat lawns. But we'll always have heroes!"

Alexandrovich Mikhalevich, dosage reader, quoted in Voices of Chernobyl.

"Since the year I was born [1986], no children have been born in our village. I was the only one. The doctors did not want my mother to have me. But she ran from the hospital and hid in her mother's house....I have no brothers or sisters. And I really want some."

Anton Nashivankin, quoted in Voices of Chernobyl.

"There was a village named Kopachi—my home. It does not exist any more. They have ruined it all with bulldozers. So I don't have a place to come back to, even if I wished to. It's a very awkward feeling—when you know that you have lost your childhood. There is no place you can show to your children. There is only this ruined reactor one kilometer north of this place."

Helena Kostuchenko, who was 19 when the accident happened. From an interview for the BBC in 2002.

Glossary

ABC suit Special clothing that protects the wearer from atomic, biological, or chemical danger.

authoritarian A term used to describe a government that expects total obedience from its citizens and will not tolerate criticism.

boron A metal-like material known for its ability to absorb radioactivity.

communist A follower of a political philosophy that believes that the state rather than private business should control the property, wealth, and resources of the country on behalf of its people.

contaminate To pollute something, such as soil or water, with a poisonous material such as radioactive waste.

coup An abbreviation of *coup d'etat*, a French phrase meaning the sudden, usually violent seizing of power in a country, often by members of the military who are determined to remove the existing government from office.

DNA Genetic material that exists in the chromosomes of all living things and carries hereditary characteristics from one generation to the next.

dolomite A rocklike material known for its ability to absorb radioactivity.

fallout Radioactivity scattered throughout an particular area following a nuclear accident or explosion.

fuel reprocessing plant A facility that takes radioactive material from nuclear power plants and treats it so that it can be used in the manufacture of nuclear weapons.

graphite A carbonlike material used in nuclear reactors to slow down nuclear reaction.

harness In this case, to control the energy of a nuclear reaction.

hydroelectric dam A barrier built across a river to harness the flow of water to produce electricity via turbines.

inflammable Something that catches fire very easily.

mental retardation Lower intelligence than normal, resulting from heredity or injury to the brain.

ministry A section of a government responsible for a particular aspect of life in that country.

monarchy A form of government that is headed by a king or queen (monarch) who has inherited this position from a former king or queen.

Nazi A follower of the German dictator Adolf Hitler, who believed that Germany should conquer Russia and other Slavic nations east of Germany; the Nazis believed themselves to be a "superior" race of people, who would dominate and enslave other "inferior" peoples.

nuclear fuel reprocessing plant *See* fuel reprocessing plant.

pile Another name for a structure of uranium and another material such as graphite, used to produce nuclear energy.

radiation plume Radioactivity scattered by the wind following a nuclear accident or explosion.

radioactive To do with radioactivity.

radioactive-contaminated The term for a material or object that gives out sufficient radiation to be harmful to living things.

radioactivity The emission of harmful rays from radioactive material such as uranium.

revolution A political situation in a country where the existing government and social structure is completely overthrown and reshaped; in the Russian Revolution of 1917, a communist regime wrested power from the monarchical ruler (the czar).

roentgens Units used to measure amounts of radiation.

scapegoat A person made to take the blame for something that should be blamed on other people or things.

tabloid A small-format newspaper, usually filled with lurid or sensational stories.

Inside the ruined Chernobyl power plant on April 29, 1986.

Further Information

Reading

Alcraft, Rob. *World's Worst Nuclear Disasters*. Chicago: Heinemann Library, 2000.

Brennan, Kristine. *The Chernobyl Nuclear Disaster*. Broomall, PA: Chelsea House Publishers, 2001.

Condon, Judith. *Chernobyl and Other Nuclear Accidents (New Perspectives)*. New York: Raintree Steck-Vaughn Publishers, 1998.

Mason, Paul. *Disaster!: In the Environment (Young Library)*. New York: Raintree Steck-Vaughn Publishers, 2002.

McQuerry, Maureen. *Nuclear Legacy: Students of Two Atomic Cities*. Columbus, Ohio: Battelle Press, 2000.

Films

Chernobyl Nuclear Disaster. MPI Home Video, 1986.

Time Line

1917 Russian Revolution. A communist regime takes control of the Russian Empire.

1922 The Russian Empire is renamed the Soviet Union.

1932 The atom is first split at Cambridge University, England.

1942 The first working nuclear reactor is tested at University of Chicago in Illinois.

August 1945 The first atomic bombs are dropped on Japan by the United States.

1951 An experimental reactor is harnessed to produce electricity at Idaho Falls, U.S.

1956 The world's first domestic nuclear power plant is opened at Calder Hall, England.

1957 A major nuclear accident occurs at a reprocessing plant near Chelyabinsk in the Soviet Union.

1972 Construction work begins on Chernobyl power plant.

1978 In the Soviet Union, Byeloyarsk reactor goes out of control following a fire.

1979 The Three Mile Island nuclear power plant disaster occurs in Pennsylvania.

1982 Fire breaks out in the No. 1 reactor at Chernobyl.

1985 Mikhail Gorbachev comes to power in the Soviet Union.

April 26, 1986 Reactor No. 4 explodes at Chernobyl.

April 27, 1986 The towns of Chernobyl and Pripyat are evacuated.

April 28, 1986 Radiation is detected in Western Europe. The Soviet authorities admit that an accident has occurred.

May 9, 1986 The fire is extinguished and the cleanup begins.

September 1986 The "sarcophagus" over reactor No. 4 is completed.

1991 Gorbachev resigns following a *coup* against him. The Soviet Union breaks up. Ukraine and Belarus become independent states.

2002 The U.S. government announces that it is resuming its nuclear-reactor building program, suspended in 1979 following the incident at Three Mile Island.

This Kiev monument to the victims of the Chernobyl explosion includes photographs of those who died during the disaster.

Index

DEMCO